The Magic of Christmas

7 Piano Duets Celebrating the Music of the Season

Dennis Alexander

Christmas is truly a time of sharing, and expressing the beauty and wonder of the Christmas season through music is an experience which provides many happy memories for years to come. These special duet arrangements are meant to please both young and old, and will provide the "perfect touch" for a Christmas recital or informal gathering. Both parts are musically interesting and rewarding to play. The words for each selection are also included so that friends and family may sing along and share the "Magic of Christmas." Have fun, and Merry Christmas to all of you!

Dennis Alexander

Second Edition
Copyright © MMVI by Alfred Publishing Co., Inc.
All Rights Reserved   Printed in USA.
ISBN-10: 0-7390-1596-6
ISBN-13: 978-7390-1596-4

Still, Still, Still

Still, still, still, He sleeps this night so chill.
The Virgin's tender arms enfolding,
Warm and safe the Child are holding,
Still, still, still, He sleeps this night so chill.

Austrian

Still, Still, Still

Still, still, still, He sleeps this night so chill.
The Virgin's tender arms enfolding,
Warm and safe the Child are holding,
Still, still, still, He sleeps this night so chill.

Andante

Austrian

Secondo

Primo

I Saw Three Ships

I saw three ships come sailing in on Christmas Day, on Christmas Day.
I saw three ships come sailing in on Christmas Day in the morning.

Allegretto

Traditional

I Saw Three Ships

I saw three ships come sailing in on Christmas Day, on Christmas Day.
I saw three ships come sailing in on Christmas Day in the morning.

Traditional

Secondo

Primo

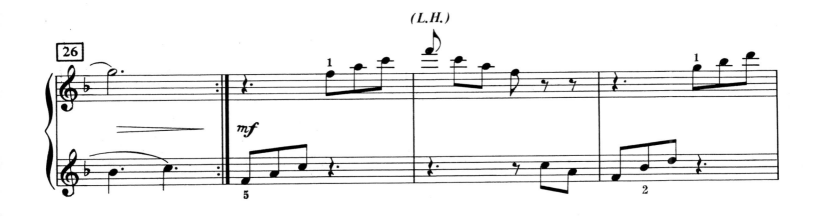

Away in a Manger

Away in a manger no crib for His bed,
The little Lord Jesus laid down His sweet head;
The stars in the sky look'd down where He lay,
The little Lord Jesus asleep on the hay.

Andante

John R. Murray

Away in a Manger

Away in a manger no crib for His bed,
The little Lord Jesus laid down His sweet head;
The stars in the sky look'd down where He lay,
The little Lord Jesus asleep on the hay.

John R. Murray

Secondo

Primo

Christmas Medley

"The Holly and the Ivy"
The holly and the ivy, when they are both fullgrown,
Of all the trees that are in the wood, the holly bears the crown.

Andante cantabile

English

Christmas Medley

"O Christmas Tree"

O Christmas Tree, O Christmas tree, with faithful leaves unchanging.
O Christmas Tree, O Christmas tree, with faithful leaves unchanging.
Not only green in summer's heat, but also winter's snow and sleet.
O Christmas tree, O Christmas tree, with faithful leaves unchanging.

German

Andante cantabile

Secondo

Primo

Secondo

Primo

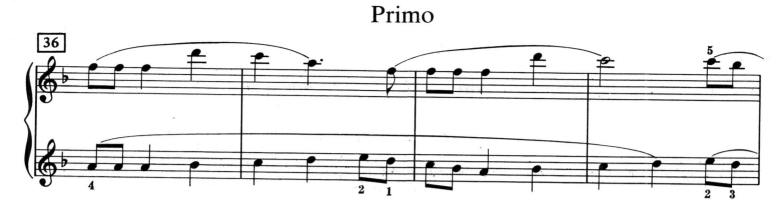

Deck the Halls

Deck the halls with boughs of holly, Fa la la la la, la la la la.
'Tis the season to be jolly, Fa la la la la, la la la la.
Don we now our gay apparel, Fa la la la la la la, la la la.
Troll the ancient Yuletide carol, Fa la la la la, la la la la.

Traditional

Deck the Halls

Deck the halls with boughs of holly, Fa la la la la, la la la la.
'Tis the season to be jolly, Fa la la la la, la la la la.
Don we now our gay apparel, Fa la la la la la la, la la la.
Troll the ancient Yuletide carol, Fa la la la la, la la la la.

Allegro

Traditional

Secondo

Primo

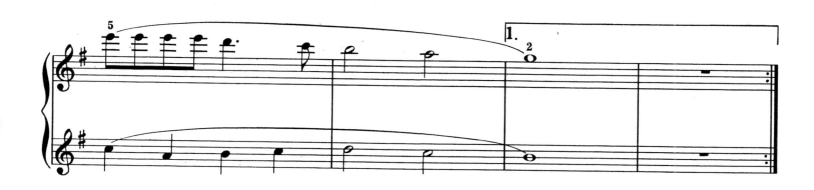

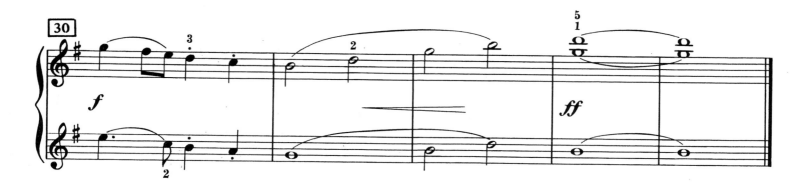

O Little Town of Bethlehem

O little town of Bethlehem, How still we see thee lie!
Above thy deep and dreamless sleep the silent stars go by;
Yet in thy dark streets shineth the everlasting Light:
The hopes and fears of all the years are met in thee tonight.

Phillips Brooks

Lewis H. Redner

O Little Town of Bethlehem

O little town of Bethlehem, How still we see thee lie!
Above thy deep and dreamless sleep the silent stars go by;
Yet in thy dark streets shineth the everlasting Light:
The hopes and fears of all the years are met in thee tonight.

Phillips Brooks

Lewis H. Redner

Secondo

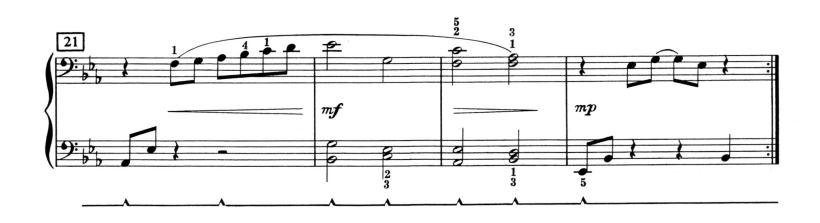

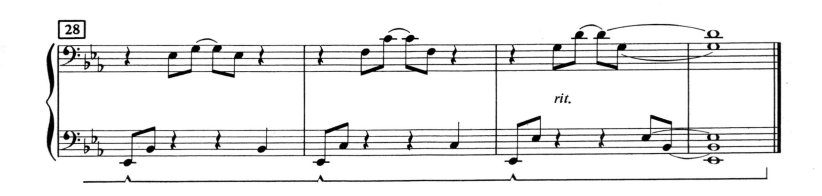

Primo

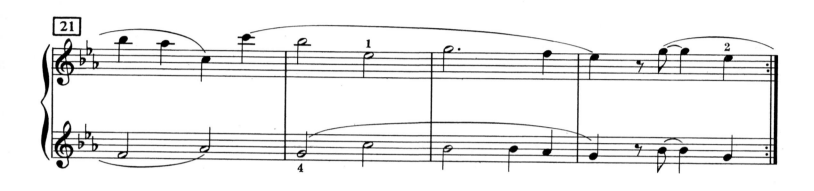

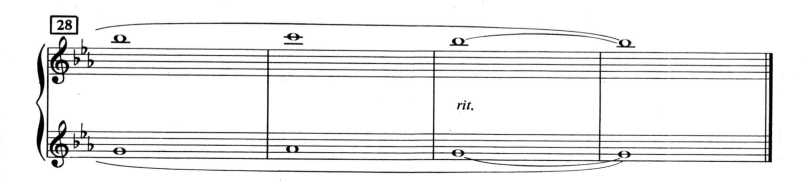

Up on the Housetop

Up on the housetop reindeer pause, Out jumps good old Santa Claus;
Down through the chimney with lots of toys, All for the little ones, Christmas joys.
Ho! Ho! Ho! Who wouldn't go; Ho! Ho! Ho! Who wouldn't go!
Up on the housetop, click, click, click,
Down through the chimney with good Saint Nick.

B. R. Hanby

Up on the Housetop

Up on the housetop reindeer pause, Out jumps good old Santa Claus;
Down through the chimney with lots of toys, All for the little ones, Christmas joys.
Ho! Ho! Ho! Who wouldn't go; Ho! Ho! Ho! Who wouldn't go!
Up on the housetop, click, click, click,
Down through the chimney with good Saint Nick.

Allegro

B. R. Hanby

Secondo

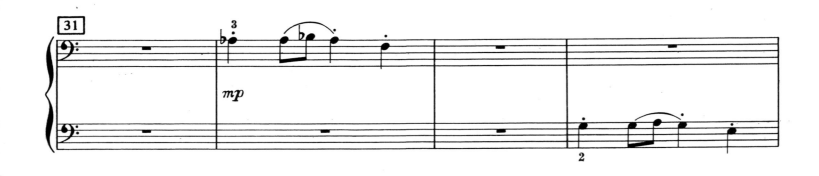

Primo

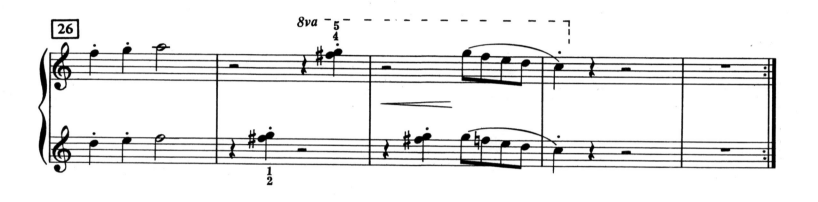

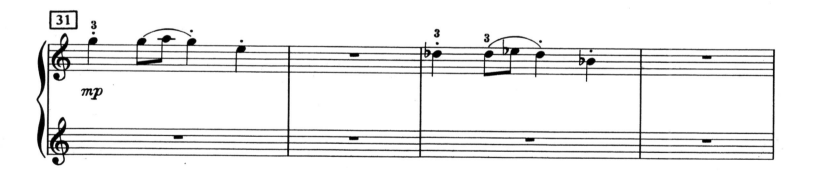